SEP 29 2014

W9-BZU-986

Drawing
Mustangs
and Other
Wild Horses

by Rae Young

CAPSTONE PRESS
a capstone imprint

Snap Books are published by Capstone Press,
1710 Roe Crest Drive, North Mankato, Minnesota 56003
www.capstonepub.com

Library of Congress Cataloging-in-Publication Data
Young, Rae.
  Drawing mustangs and other wild horses / by Rae Young.
      pages cm. — (Snap. Drawing horses)
  Summary: "Lively text and step-by-step instructions give an introduction to drawing horses"— Provided by publisher.
  ISBN 978-1-4765-4002-3 (library binding)
  ISBN 978-1-4765-6052-6 (eBook PDF)
1. Horses in art—Juvenile literature. 2. Mustang—Juvenile literature.
3. Wild horses—Juvenile literature. 4. Drawing—Technique--Juvenile literature. I. Title.
  NC783.8.H65Y682 2014d
  743.6'96655—dc23   2013035802

Editorial Credits
Mari Bolte, editor; Lori Bye, designer; Jennifer Walker, production specialist

Photo Credits
All illustrations are by Q2AMedia Services Private Ltd, except for June Brigman, 28-29, 30-31

Printed in China by Nordica.
1013/CA21301921
092013   007745NORDS14

TABLE OF CONTENTS

Getting Started 4

Tools of the Trade.......................... 5

Hover Pony.......................... 6

Running Around.......................... 8

Splish Splash.......................... 10

Long Day.......................... 12

Not Quite Misty.......................... 14

Down Under 16

A Bit Dusty 18

Mini Donkey 20

Out West.......................... 22

Chasing Cows 24

Bucking Pony.......................... 26

Afternoon Nap.......................... 28

Saddled With Spots.......................... 30

Internet Sites 32

Look For All the Books in This Series....... 32

GETTING STARTED

Some artists see the world as their canvas. Others see the world as their pasture! If you're a horse lover, grab a pencil and a notebook. Just pick a project and follow the step-by-step instructions. Even if you've never drawn a horse before, the projects in this book will get you started. You'll have everything you need to draw a funny foal or a record-setting racehorse.

Once you've mastered the basics, try giving your art a personal touch. Customize each horse's saddle pad or halter with bright colors and patterns. Add in details like silver conchos or textured leather. Draw accessories such as winter blankets, first-place ribbons, or buckets and brushes. Why not try drawing your friends on a trail ride or galloping across a beach? Don't be afraid to get creative!

TOOLS OF THE TRADE

1 Every artist needs something to draw on. Clean white paper is perfect for creating art. Use a drawing pad or a folder to organize your artwork.

2 Pencils are great for both simple sketches and difficult drawings. Always have one handy!

3 Finish your drawing with color! Colored pencils, markers, or even paints give your equine art detail and realism.

4 Want to add more finishing touches? Try outlining and shading your drawings with artist pens.

5 Don't be afraid of digital art! There are lots of free or inexpensive drawing apps for tablets or smartphones. Apps are a great way to experiment with different tools while on the go.

HOVER PONY

Some people describe a horse bucking or galloping with all four legs off the ground as a "hover pony." Draw this hover pony performing its own airs above the ground!

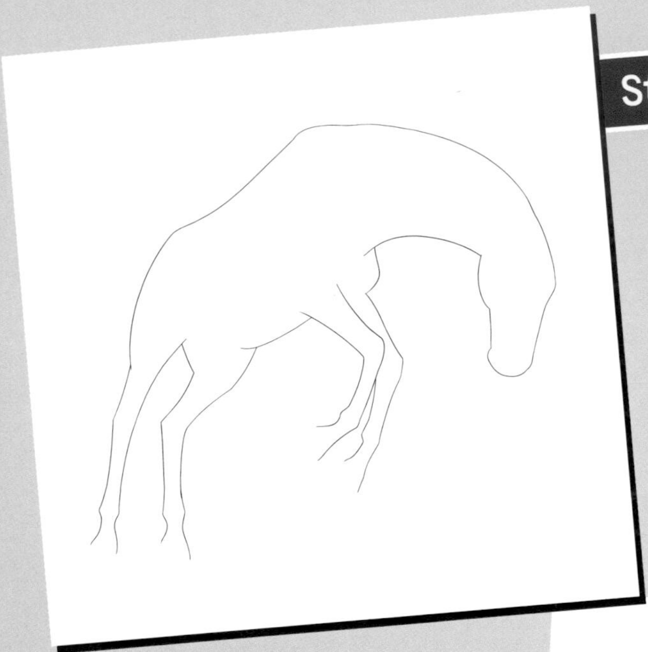

Step 1.

Tip

This horse is perlino. Perlino horses have white or light cream bodies. Their manes and tails are darker and have reddish hairs. They have pink skin and blue eyes.

Step 2.

Step 3.

Step 4.

RUNNING AROUND

In the wild, horses travel between 10 and 20 miles (16 and 32 kilometers) a day. But domestic horses like this one don't have that much room to move around. Instead, they burn off extra energy through play. Bucking and galloping in a pasture gives a horse time to just be a horse!

Step 1.

Tip

Draw this horse a friend! A mule, dog, cat, cow, or even another horse would be a great playmate.

Step 2.

Step 3.

Step 4.

9

SPLISH SPLASH

Horses love to have fun! Some, like this horse, really enjoy playing in water. They like to paw, splash, and roll! Some mischievous horses will dunk their food or tip their water buckets over.

Step 1.

Step 2.

Tip

Plants and animals can make your pond come alive! Try adding ducks, lily pads, fish, or frogs.

LONG DAY

Horses spend anywhere from four to 14 hours resting each day. They may sleep for a few minutes or a few hours at a time. Like humans, horses yawn for a variety of reasons. A yawning horse may be relaxed or stretching its face muscles.

Step 1.

Step 2.

Tip

Draw the rest of this horse's body. Don't be afraid to draw it sleeping! Their legs lock, preventing them from falling over while relaxed or sleeping.

Step 3.

Step 4.

NOT QUITE MISTY

Chincoteague ponies run wild off the coast of Virginia. Despite their name, they actually live on the neighboring island of Assateague. They have lived there for more than 200 years. It is believed that the ponies are descendants of horses who survived the sinking of a Spanish ship. Every year the island's two herds swim to Chincoteague.

Tip

Chincoteague ponies drink salt water. This gives their bodies a round appearance. Be sure to make your pony roly-poly!

Step 1.

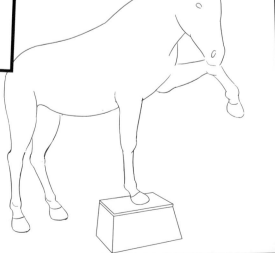

Step 2.

14

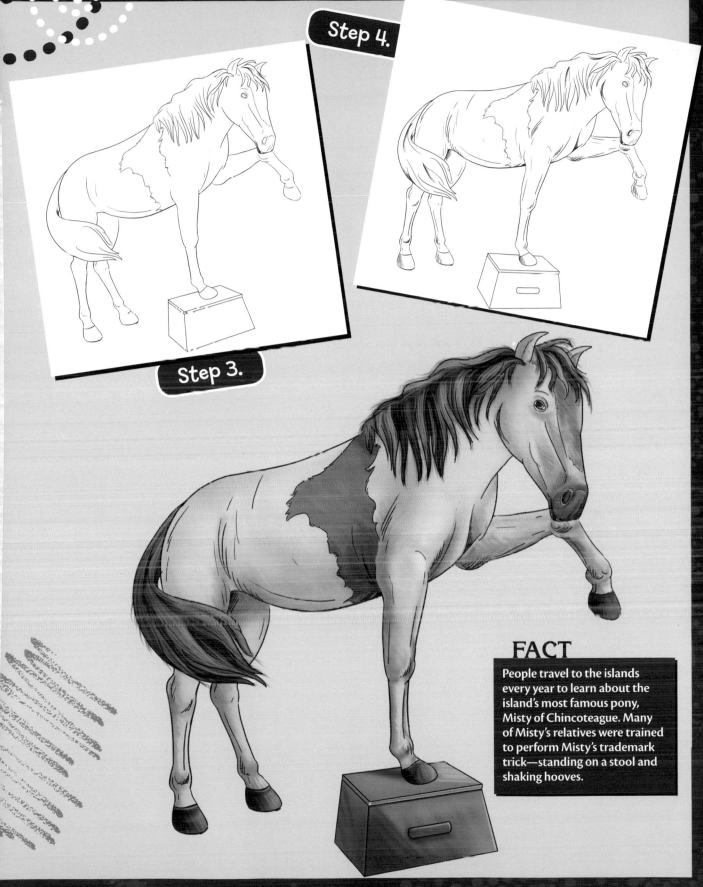

Step 4.

Step 3.

FACT

People travel to the islands every year to learn about the island's most famous pony, Misty of Chincoteague. Many of Misty's relatives were trained to perform Misty's trademark trick—standing on a stool and shaking hooves.

DOWN UNDER

An Australian horse needs an Australian saddle! The lightweight Australian saddle is most similar to a dressage saddle. Its long flaps give a rider close contact with the horse. The deep seat helps a rider feel safe over dangerous footing.

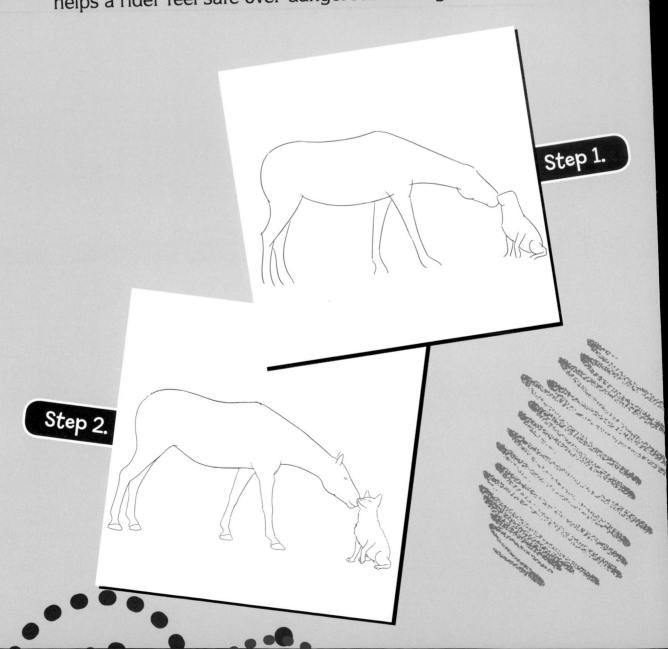

Step 1.

Step 2.

Step 3.

Step 4.

Tip

The Australian stock horse is a versatile breed. Some call it "the breed for every need." Draw your stock horse cutting cattle, competing on the trail, or competing at a rodeo.

17

A BIT DUSTY

Horses roll for a variety of reasons. Some might use dust or dirt as protection from the hot sun or biting insects. Others might enjoy rolling after a bath, to dry their coats faster. Some, like this horse, might just have an itch!

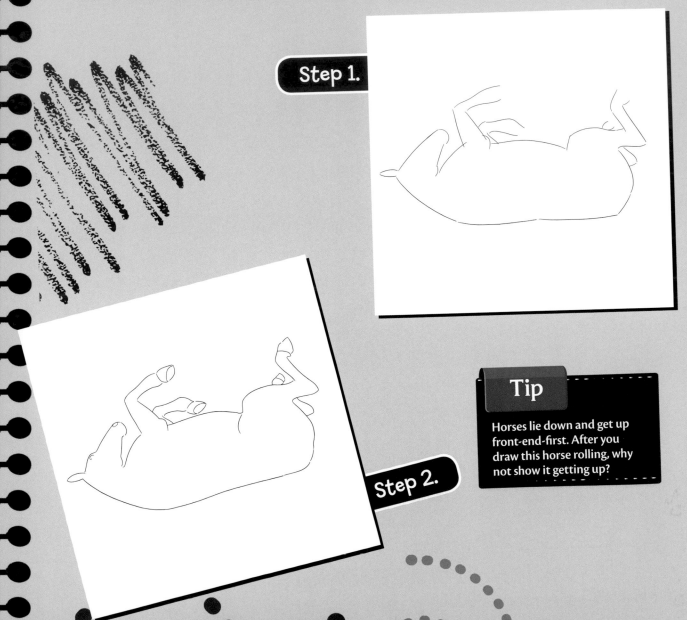

Step 1.

Step 2.

Tip

Horses lie down and get up front-end-first. After you draw this horse rolling, why not show it getting up?

Step 3.

Step 4.

MINI DONKEY

Donkeys are part of the horse family but are a different species. Like mules, donkeys come in all sizes. Miniature donkeys are popular as companion animals. They stand at 36 inches (90 centimeters) and under.

Step 1.

Tip

Try drawing this donkey in various sizes. How would it look drawn as a regular-sized horse? Would it look different if it were the size of a draft horse?

Step 2.

Step 3.

Step 4.

OUT WEST

Mustangs have done more than wander the plains. They have also been used on ranches for generations. Their thick skin and sturdy hooves make them the ideal cow horse. Mustangs come in any color, so get creative!

Step 1.

Step 2.

FACT

In 1971 Congress named wild horses and burros as living symbols of the American West. Today the Bureau of Land Management (BLM) estimates that more than 37,000 wild horses and burros roam over 10 states.

Step 3.

Step 4.

CHASING COWS

Got cow? The quarter horse has worked on American ranches for generations. A horse with good cow sense has a strong drive to cut a single cow from a herd of cattle. Cutting horses work on ranches and compete at horse shows. A good cutting horse has speed, flexibility, and a natural instinct to move with cattle.

Step 1.

Step 2.

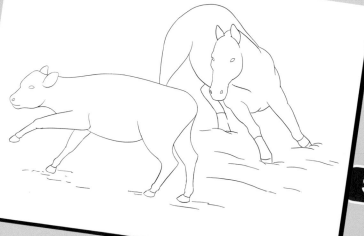

FACT

Quarter horses are sometimes called stock horses. Other stock horse breeds include appaloosas and paint horses. Add a splash of white to your cutting horse to turn it into another stock horse breed.

Step 4.

Step 3.

BUCKING PONY

Ponies are known to be mischievous. A bucking pony may be blowing off steam or showing its playful side. Or it could be getting rid of its rider!

Step 1.

FACT

Professional bucking horses, like those you see in rodeos, often come from long lines of proven buckers.

Step 2.

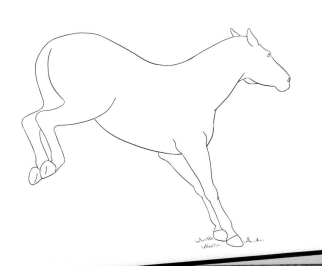

Step 4.

AFTERNOON NAP

Horses can't get up as fast as people. In the wild, a horse caught off its feet might be an easy target for predators. Horses usually sleep standing up. When they feel safe, they might nap lying down.

Step 1.

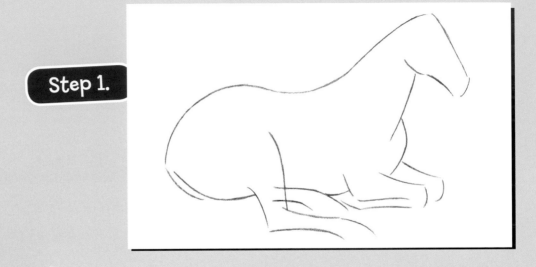

Step 2.

Step 3.

Step 4.

FACT

Horses have a special system in their bodies. This system allows them to sleep standing up without falling over. Horses can stay standing for as long as three years without lying down!

SADDLED WITH SPOTS

Appaloosas' spotted coats make them a recognizable breed. In addition to spots, they also have striped hooves, patchy-colored skin, and white circles around their eyes.

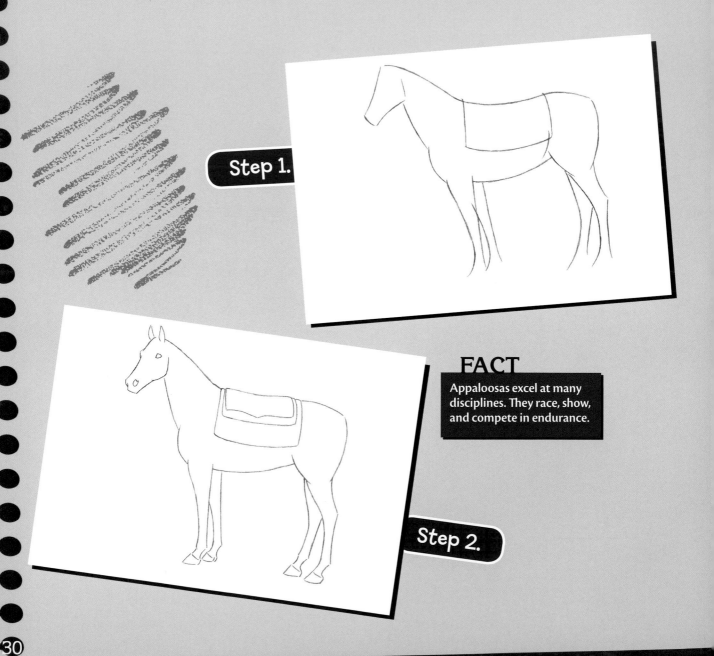

Step 1.

Step 2.

FACT

Appaloosas excel at many disciplines. They race, show, and compete in endurance.

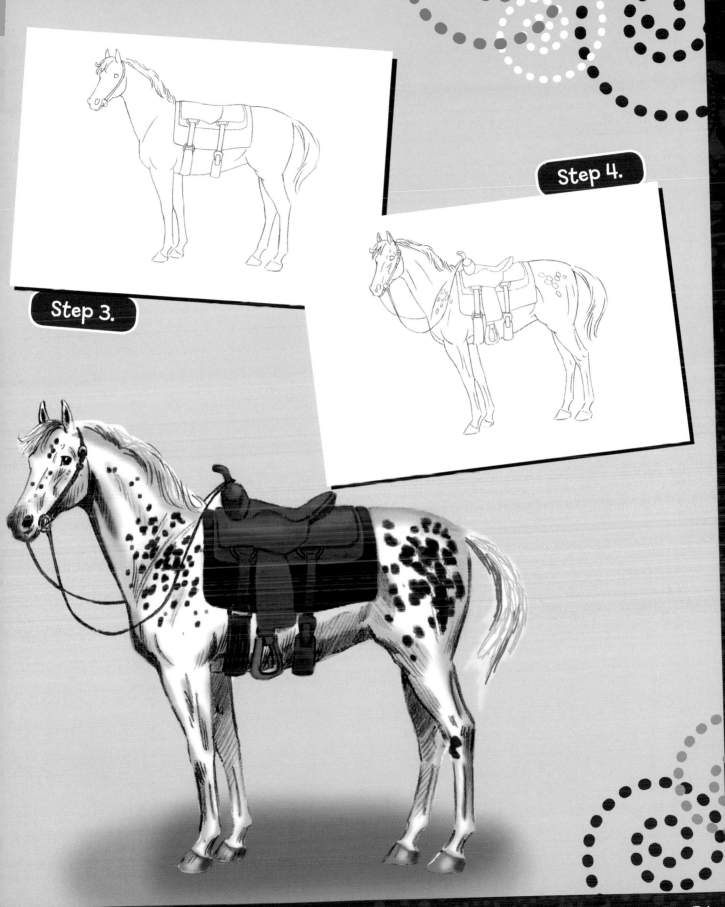

INTERNET SITES

FactHound offers a safe, fun way to find Internet sites related to this book. All of the sites on FactHound have been researched by our staff.

Here's all you do:

Visit *www.facthound.com*

Type in this code: 9781476540023

 Check out projects, games and lots more at
www.capstonekids.com

LOOK FOR ALL THE BOOKS IN THIS SERIES

Drawing Appaloosas and Other Handsome Horses

Drawing Friesians and Other Beautiful Horses

Drawing Arabians and Other Amazing Horses

Drawing Mustangs and Other Wild Horses

Drawing Barrel Racers and Other Speedy Horses

Drawing Thoroughbreds and Other Elegant Horses